Earth's Weather and Seasons

by Ann J. Jacobs

PEARSON

Scott
Foresman

DK

What are some kinds of weather?

You wake up.
How do you know what to put on?
Check the weather!

Weather is what it is like outside.
Is it hot, or is it cold?
Look up at the sky.
Look at the tree branches.
Are they moving?
Is there wind?

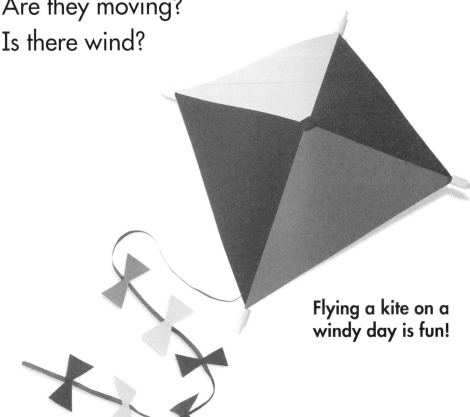

Flying a kite on a windy day is fun!

Wet and Dry Weather

Rain, sleet, and snow are all wet weather. Clouds help tell what kind of weather is coming.
Clouds are made of many drops of water. The drops grow larger and then fall.

Heavy rains can fall in spring and summer.

Water from clouds can fall as rain, snow, or sleet.
Snow and sleet fall when the air is cold.
Rain falls when the air is warm.

Sometimes rain does not fall for a long time.
This is called a drought.
There is no water for plants and animals when this happens.

Some plants cannot live in a drought.

Some places get snow in winter.

What is the water cycle?

Water moves between the land and the sky.
This is called the **water cycle.**
Water falls from clouds to Earth's surface.
Then it moves back up to the clouds.
Look at the four steps of the water cycle.

1. Water falls from the clouds. It can be rain, snow, or sleet.

2. Water goes into rivers, lakes, and oceans.

3. The Sun makes some of the water **evaporate.** It changes into water vapor.

4. Water vapor gets cold.
   It condenses into clouds.
   Condense means to change
   back into drops of water.

What is spring?

Weather can change with the seasons.

Some spring days are cool.
Some spring days are warm or rainy.
Plants grow in the spring.
Many animals have babies.

**A deer and her
baby in the spring.**

What is summer?

Summer comes after spring.
Summer can have hot days and
warm nights.
Green leaves grow on many trees
and plants.
Flowers, fruits, and vegetables grow.

You can see animal
families in the summer.

What is fall?

Fall comes after summer.
In fall the air gets cooler.
Some leaves change colors.

Some animals look for food for the winter.
Other animals **migrate,** or go to a
different place.

In fall, some animals find food for the winter.

What is winter?

Winter comes after fall.
Winter can be very cold.
It may snow.
Ponds and streams may turn to ice.

Some animals **hibernate.**
They sleep all winter and wake up in
the spring.

**Bears hibernate
in the winter.**

What are some kinds of bad weather?

A thunderstorm is one kind of bad weather.
A thunderstorm has lots of wind and rain.
A thunderstorm has thunder.
It has lightning.
Lightning is a flash of light in the sky.

Thunderstorm Safety!

- Go inside.

- Keep away from water.

- Keep away from things made of metal.

- Do not stand under a tree.

- Do not use a phone.

- Keep away from electrical things.

Tornadoes

A **tornado** is a very strong wind.
A tornado comes down from the clouds.
It looks like a funnel.

A tornado breaks everything in its path.

Tornado Safety!

- Get inside a closet or a bathroom.

- Sit under the stairs.

- Keep away from windows.

- Keep away from water.

- Keep away from things made of metal and things that are electric.

- Cover your head.

- If you are outside, lie flat on the ground.

Hurricanes

A **hurricane** is a big storm.
A hurricane starts over warm ocean water.
The rain from a hurricane can make a flood.

A hurricane has strong winds.
The winds can blow down trees and buildings.

Hurricane Safety!

- Move to a place away from the ocean.

- Cover up windows.

- Bring things inside.

- Keep drinking water with you.

- Make sure your flashlight and radio work.

- Stay inside.

- Stay away from windows.

Weather changes from season to season.
Some weather is wet.
Some weather is dry.
Some weather is hot.
Some weather is cold.

Some weather is not safe.
Some weather is fun.

What is the weather like today?

Glossary

condense   to change into small drops of water

evaporate   to change into water vapor

hibernate   to have a long, deep sleep during winter

hurricane   a strong windstorm that starts over warm ocean water

lightning   a flash of light in the sky

migrate   to move to a warmer place

tornado   a strong wind that comes down from the clouds

water cycle   the way water moves from the clouds to Earth and back to the clouds